The World's Best Blonde Jokes

Compiled by Laura Crenshaw
Illustrated by April Stokes

Peroxide Press
Chapel Hill, North Carolina

Copyright © 1992 by Laura Crenshaw
Illustrations Copyright © 1992 by April Stokes
All rights reserved.

Printed in the United States of America

ISBN 0-9632280-0-5

Peroxide Press
P.O. Box 3051
Chapel Hill, NC 27515

To Anna

Acknowledgements

Thanks to Lisa Clyburn, Claire Crenshaw, Scott Crenshaw, Blake Dickinson, Jill Doss, Fred Good, Jan Elliott, Chuck Haymes, Freddy Hill, Doug Hoogervorst, Susan Margolis, Scott Maxwell, Lisa Reiners, Jacqui Ressler, Mark Schultz, James Sutton and Jerry Van Sant for jokes, advice and other support.

What does a blonde call her pet zebra?
Spot.

— ◇ —

What goes vroom, screech, vroom, screech?
A blonde going through a flashing red light.

— ◇ —

What does a blonde say when you ask her if her blinker is on?
"It's on. It's off. It's on. It's off."

Why don't blondes like to make Kool-Aid?
They can't fit eight cups of water in the little packet.

— ◊ —

Did you hear about the blonde who shot the arrow straight up in the air?
She missed.

— ◊ —

What did the blonde think of the new computer?
She didn't like it because she couldn't get channel 9.

How does a blonde turn on the light after sex?
She opens the car door.

What do blondes and cow pies have in common?
The older they get, the easier they are to pick up.

Why do blondes like tilt steering wheels?
More headroom.

How do you get a blonde to marry you?
Tell her she's pregnant.

Why don't blondes eat pickles?

They get their heads stuck in the jar.

The jars have lids, not zippers.

What's it called when one blonde blows in another blonde's ear?
Data transfer.

Why do blondes write "TGIF" on their tennis shoes?
"Toes Go In First"

How do blonde brain cells die?
Alone.

— ◇ —

How do you give a blonde a brain transplant?
Blow in her ear.

— ◇ —

Why do blondes wash their hair in the sink?
That's where you wash vegetables.

What do blondes and beer bottles have in common?
They're both empty from the neck up.

What do a blonde and Gorbachev have in common?
They both got screwed by 10 men while on vacation.

What's the difference between a blonde and Gorbachev?
Gorbachev knew who the ten men were.

Why are all blonde jokes one-liners?
So men can understand them.

How can you tell when a blonde has been using your computer?
There's White-Out on the screen.

How can you tell when a blonde had a bad day?
She has a tampon behind her ear and she doesn't know what she did with her pencil.

What did the blonde do before taking a urine test?
Study.

Why do blondes take the pill?
So they know what day of the week it is.

What do you call a brunette and two blondes?
Regular price, four bucks, four bucks.

What's the advantage of being married to a blonde?
You can park in handicapped zones.

— ◇ —

What does a blonde say after multiple orgasms?
"Way to go, team!"

— ◇ —

What happens when a blonde gets Alzheimer's disease?
Her IQ goes up.

What do you call a brunette standing between two blondes?
An interpreter.

How can you tell if a blonde owns a vibrator?
She has chipped teeth.

— ◇ —

Why do blondes have so much free time?
Because so little is expected of them.

— ◇ —

What's the difference between a smart blonde and Bigfoot?
Bigfoot's been spotted.

How do you keep a baby blonde amused?
Give her a mirror and some makeup.

How many blondes does it take to make chocolate-chip cookies?
Three. One to mix the batter, two to peel the M&Ms.

— ◇ —

How do you drive a blonde insane?
Ask her to alphabetize your M&Ms.

— ◇ —

Why was the blonde fired from the M&M factory?
She kept throwing out all the Ws.

Why is it so difficult to teach a blonde to drive?

She keeps getting in the back seat.

She can't reach the pedals from the back seat.

She thinks the steering wheel is a clothes rack.

What's the difference between a blonde and a guy?
The blonde has a higher sperm count.

What do you call 10 blondes standing shoulder-to-shoulder?
A wind tunnel.

What did the blonde take to her make-up exam?
Her cosmetics.

— ◊ —

Why do blondes wear underwear.
Because they make good ankle warmers.

— ◊ —

Why was the blonde depressed after she got her driver's license?
Because she got an F in sex.

What did the blonde have tattooed on her inner thigh?
"Welcome home, 1st Battalion."

What's the difference between a blonde and a Ferrari?

You probably can find a guy who hasn't been in a Ferrari.

Why did the blonde have a sore belly button?

Her boyfriend was blonde, too.

What's the best way to drown a blonde?
Put a mirror on the bottom of a swimming pool.

How many blondes does it take to screw in a lightbulb?

What's a lightbulb?

None. They only screw in cars.

One. She holds the bulb and the world revolves around her.

Two. One to hold the Diet Pepsi, one to call "Daaaaady!"

What does a blonde say after you blow into her ear?
Thanks for the refill.

Santa Claus, the tooth fairy, a smart blonde and a dumb blonde are walking down the street when they spot a $10 bill. Who picks it up?

The dumb blonde. There's no such thing as Santa Claus, the tooth fairy or a smart blonde.

A brunette and a blonde are walking in a park. The brunette suddenly says, "Aww, look at the dead bird." The blonde stops, looks up and says, "Where?"

How does a blonde know when she's slept with an elephant?

The smell of peanuts on his breath.

She's pregnant for 23 months.

The big "E" on his pajamas.

What do you call a blonde with half a brain?
Gifted.

What do you call 15 blondes standing in a circle?
A dope ring.

Did you hear about the blonde who liked younger men?

She started sleeping with Cub Scouts, but her doctor made her stop when she got up to three Packs a day.

Is it true that blondes have more fun?

No, but their boyfriends do.

If Tarzan and Jane were blondes, what would Cheetah be?
The smartest of the three.

What would have happened if Pee Wee Herman were blonde?
He would have had something better in his hand.

— ◇ —

Did you hear about the blonde guy whose wife gave birth to twins?
He wanted to know who the other man was.

What do you call it when a blonde dyes her hair brunette?
Artificial intelligence.

Why do blondes wear shoulder pads?
(while rocking head from side to side) "I don't know."

How do you kill a blonde?
Put spikes in her shoulder pads.

How do blondes pierce their ears?
They put tacks in their shoulder pads.

How do you make a blonde's eyes sparkle?
Shine a flashlight in her ear.

What do blondes put behind their ears to attract men?
Their legs.

Why do blondes wear green lipstick?
Because red means stop.

What did the blonde's mother say before her date?
"If you're not in bed by 12, come home."

What's the first thing a blonde does in the morning?

Introduces herself.

Goes home.

A blonde and a brunette jump off a 20-story building. Who hits the ground first?

The brunette. The blonde has to stop for directions.

Why did the blonde have square breasts?
She forgot to take the tissue out of the box.

What's the mating call of the blonde?
"I'm sooooo drunk."

What's the mating call of the ugly blonde?
"I said, I'm drunk!"

What's the mating call of the brunette?
"Have all the blondes gone home yet?"

What's the mating call of the red-head?
"Next!"

Why should blondes not be given coffee breaks.
It takes so long to retrain them.

What did the blonde say when she looked in a box of Cheerios?
"Oh look! Donut seeds!"

Why don't blondes like PMS?
Because they can't spell it.

How did the blonde try to kill a bird?
She threw it off a cliff.

How many blondes does it take to make popcorn?
Five. One to hold the kettle, four to shake the stove.

What do you say to a blonde who won't give in?
"Have another beer."

Why do blondes have more fun?
Because they don't know any better.

What do you call a blonde skeleton in the closet?
Last year's hide-and-seek champ.

Why do blondes tease their hair?
To catch everything that goes over their heads.

Two blondes are in a parking lot trying to unlock the door of their convertible with a coat hanger. The first blonde says, "I can't get this door unlocked!" The second blonde says, "Hurry up and try harder. It's starting to rain and the top's down!"

Two blondes were walking through the woods when they saw a set of tracks. The first blonde said, "Those look like bear tracks!" The second blonde said, "No, no. Those are moose tracks." Then the train hit them.

What do you call 10 blondes in a freezer?
Frosted Flakes.

What does a blonde say when she gives birth?
"Gee, are you sure it's mine?"

— ◊ —

Why did the blonde get so excited after she finished her jigsaw puzzle in only six months?
Because the box said "From 2 to 4 years."

— ◊ —

Why do blondes always die before help arrives?
They always forget the 11 in 911.

What do brunettes do on Saturday nights?
Wish they were blonde.

About the Authors

Like most blondes, they were born brunettes.

To order additional copies of **The World's Best Blonde Jokes**, send $4.95 plus $1 shipping and handling to:
Peroxide Press
P.O. Box 3051
Chapel Hill, NC 27515

(N.C. residents please add 30¢ sales tax)

Or ask your local bookseller to carry this book.
Quantity discounts available.